Sign Language
& Numbers

Bela Davis

Abdo Kids Junior
is an Imprint of Abdo Kids
abdobooks.com

Abdo

EVERYDAY SIGN LANGUAGE

Kids

abdobooks.com

Published by Abdo Kids, a division of ABDO, P.O. Box 398166, Minneapolis, Minnesota 55439.
Copyright © 2023 by Abdo Consulting Group, Inc. International copyrights reserved in all countries.
No part of this book may be reproduced in any form without written permission from the publisher.
Abdo Kids Junior™ is a trademark and logo of Abdo Kids.

Printed in the United States of America, North Mankato, Minnesota.

102022

012023

 THIS BOOK CONTAINS
RECYCLED MATERIALS

Photo Credits: Shutterstock

Production Contributors: Teddy Borth, Jennie Forsberg, Grace Hansen

Design Contributors: Candice Keimig, Pakou Moua

Library of Congress Control Number: 2022937172

Publisher's Cataloging-in-Publication Data

Names: Davis, Bela, author.

Title: Sign language & numbers / by Bela Davis

Description: Minneapolis, Minnesota : Abdo Kids, 2023 | Series: Everyday sign language | Includes online
    resources and index.

Identifiers: ISBN 9781098264086 (lib. bdg.) | ISBN 9781098264642 (ebook) | ISBN 9781098264925
    (Read-to-Me ebook)

Subjects: LCSH: American Sign Language--Juvenile literature. | Counting--Juvenile literature. | Deaf--
    Means of communication--Juvenile literature. | Language acquisition--Juvenile literature.

Classification: DDC 419--dc23

Table of Contents

Signs and Numbers

ASL is a visual language. There is a sign for every number!

NUMBER

1. Pinch the fingers and thumb of each hand together to form bent "O" hands
2. Touch the tips of the fingers together
3. Separate the hands, twist them, and touch fingertips again

The happy cake has
one candle.

ONE

Palm faces body

The cute puppy has
two **floppy** ears.

TWO

Palm faces body

9

The monster with three eyes is sad. The monster with four eyes is glad!

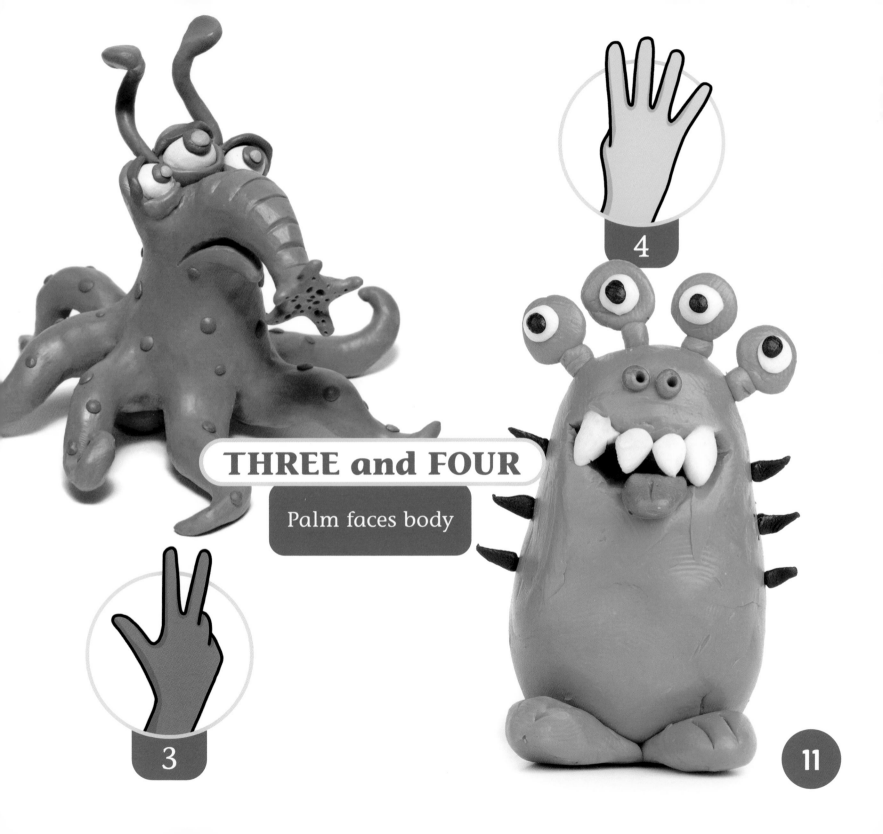

THREE and FOUR

Palm faces body

4

3

Five cute ducklings **waddle** around.

Six cute kittens sit in cups.

SIX

Palm faces forward

There are seven

yummy donuts!

SEVEN

Palm faces forward

Eight hot air balloons
float in the air.

EIGHT

Palm faces forward

There are nine spooky
pumpkins. There are
ten flying bats.

NINE and TEN

Nine: Palm faces forward
Ten: Twist hand and wrist
back and forth

10

9

The ASL Alphabet!

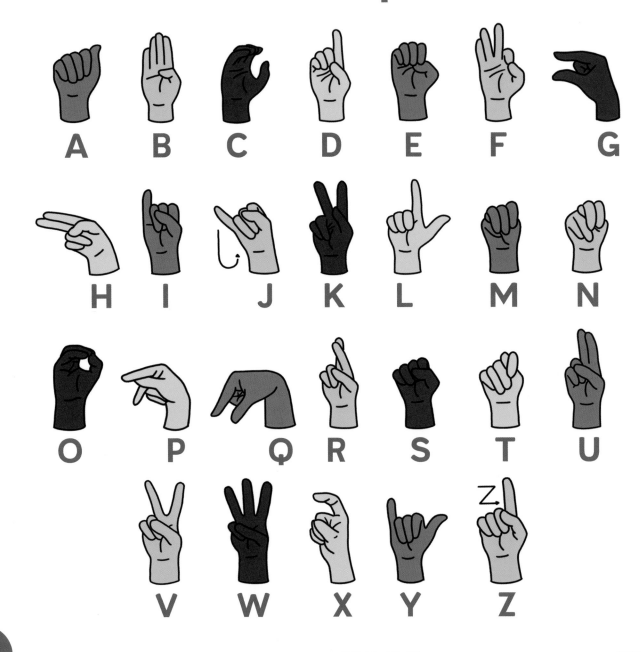

Glossary

floppy
hanging or flopping in a loose way.

ASL
short for American Sign Language, a language used by many deaf people in North America.

waddle
to walk using short steps while rocking from side to side.

Index

Abdo Kids
ONLINE
FREE! ONLINE MULTIMEDIA RESOURCES

Visit **abdokids.com** to access crafts, games, videos, and more!

Use Abdo Kids code
ESK4086
or scan this QR code!